The Ch Hïppïe

Sarah L. Bowman

Cover Art and photography by:

Mae Ann Photography Of Belleville Michigan
http://www.MaeAnnPhotography.com

Soft cover Printed in The United States of America

9781973161684

Free Faith Publishing

Sarah Bowman

Dedication

This book is dedicated to my beautiful daughters and my loving husband. You have taught me more than you will ever know. Most importantly, I thank my Lord and Savior Jesus Christ for dying on the cross, for such a sinner as I. He teaches me and shows me every day, that I am so very loved and cherished by a merciful and beautiful savior. He loves me and loves you too. Yea, though I walk through the valley of the shadow of death: I will fear no evil; for thou art with me; thy rod and thy staff, they comfort me. You have been here my whole life, my faithful friend my Lord Jesus Christ!

Sarah Bowman

Peace

Finding peace among God's creation. When was the last
time You took a moment to appreciate the beauty around you?

To just be thankful, where you are at that this second. You

may be facing significant hurdles today. However, you have

that one moment of freedom. Perhaps, if you are able, you

should take a small walk, look up at the sky, and realize that

you were created for greatness. No matter what obstacles you

are facing at this moment.

God created you for greatness. Taking the time, to just be

present, in the moment, take time, to be thankful for the breath

that is in your lungs. Everything, is okay, at this moment.

4

Sarah Bowman

The Christian Hippie

Calm, the racing thoughts in your mind, just focusing on the good around you! The blessing of your eyes, being able to see, or the gift of the ears being able to hear a bluebird pass by your window.

Our minds focus on so much negative, that it cancels out, the positive in our life! If you have to make a list of the positive, so you can start living in the moment then do so! Do whatever, you can to make the minutes count. Life, passes by so quickly, that we often just forget to live! We just go through the motions, of life on auto-piolet. Never really appreciating the moments, in our life until they're gone I know that this life is full of trials, and there are so many sad moments. I have walked through many of these trials.

However, being alive offers us so much glorious moments. You have been created for greatness, you can always, start over. If God gives you another day, and you open your eyes. You get a re-do. Take some time today, to focus on the good, the pure and the lovely. You can even raise your hands to the sky, giving thanks for the moment of clarity, and peace! For

Sarah Bowman

God, knows your troubles, and he will gladly carry them if you ask. There are moments in our life; we just have to surrender, to the God, that knows our name. Wherever you're at, in this journey. Know that God desires a relationship with you! He created you for greatness! Just be still.

Troubles may come your way, however at that moment. You have the breath in your lungs, the beating of your heart in your chest. So, you are okay, just close your eyes, and just be okay. It's okay, to just breath, it's okay to just be.

Sarah Bowman

Be still

It is in my quietness; I seek your face as my spirit connects with you in that space. When I am alone with you and as I quietly gaze upon the beauty of your magnificent creation. I watch as your creation speaks of your perfection, your patience and your love!

My Dearest Creator, my gracious and loving father. Could I sit with you for a moment? Sit with you amongst the trees, as I breathe in the earth around me. I find refuge here; I find peace, and harmony among the green. When I am alone in your magnificent creation, I feel close to you. The bowing of the trees, speak your name as they reach swaying towards the warmth of the sun. There is no other place, which I would rather be. Alone with you my dear Lord. I find peace within the blades of grass; you planted the seeds, my holy God. The

Sarah Bowman

seeds grow, towards the warmth of the heavenly sun. I am at peace, with you my God. I feel secure here, in your world.

The dirt beneath my feet, yielding the beauty of your creation. As the Ivy twists and turns, praising your creation. The earth cries out, its branches, towards the holy creator. All of the creation is named perfectly.

I can see your fingerprints along the whitewashed clouds. Your masterpiece, as you spoke the earth into existence, with just the sound of your voice.

It carries Lord, above the mountains so high, Lord it moves along the edge of the sky, as the clouds join. It carries Lord, to the green valleys, which are lush and alive. It carries Lord, flowing towards the highest peak; it carries Lord, beneath the sea. You are here Lord, your art. You have created us a beautiful world. I worship, you dear Lord. I hear your whispers, through my soul. I can understand your whisper in my ear, God. You are there inside of your creation, your work,

Sarah Bowman

your nature. You are the sun, you are the moon, and you are everything because you are God! The one and only God!

The trees hear your voice; they bend and sway in your presence. Your beautiful creation declares your glory. The way the sun peaks behind a cloud at just the right moment. They know their creator exists. The distant sound of the pond frog. They communicate with you, their creator.

We are your perfect creation. We are complete in your sight. The growing of the flowers, they reach towards you, gracious father. They grow to impress you, Lord, all creation was in your plan. We were all in your plan, us Lord, and we too were in your plan. In the beginning, God created the heaven and the earth, and the earth was without form and void; and darkness was upon the face of the deep. The Spirit of God moved upon the face of the waters. God said let there be light, and there was indeed light. God saw that the light was good. He then divided the light from darkness. God called the light the day, and the darkness he called night. God made the firmament and divided the waters, which were above the firmament, and

Sarah Bowman

it was so. God called the firmament heaven. The evening and the morning was the second day.

My highest God. Your Spirit always existed. God said let waters in heaven gather unto one place, and let the dry land appear: and it was so. And God called the dry land Earth, and the gathering together of the waters he called the Seas, And God saw that this was good. And God said let the earth bring forth grass, the herb yielding seed and the fruit after his kind and the tree yielding fruit after his kind, whose seed is in itself, upon the Earth and God saw that this was good. Let me see, Lord as you build our creation. I'm in wonder, as I gaze at the trees, knowing your voice, spoke the very trees alive! And the evening and the morning was the third day. And God said let there be lights in the firmament of the heaven to divide the day from the night, and let them signs, and for seasons, and for days, and for years. And let them be for lights in the firmament of the heavens to give light to the earth.

And to rule over the day and the night, and to divide the light from darkness, and God saw that is was good. And the

Sarah Bowman

evening and the morning were the fourth day. And God said let, the waters bring forth abundantly the moving creature that hath life and the fowl that may fly above the earth in the open firmament of heaven.

God created great whales and every living creature that moveth, which waters brought forth abundantly, after their kind, and every winged fowl; after its kind: And God saw that it was good.

God blessed them saying, be fruitful and multiply, and fill the waters in the Sea, and let the fowl, multiply the earth. And the evening and the morning were the fifth day! God said, let us make man in our image, after our own likeness; and let them have dominion over the fish of the sea and over the fowl of the air, and over the cattle, and over the earth, and over every creeping thing that creepeth upon the earth.

So, God created man in his own image, in the image of God created him and female he created he them. And God blessed them, and God said, unto them, be fruitful and multiply and

11

Sarah Bowman

replenish the earth and subdue it; and have dominion over the fish of the sea and over the fowl of the air.

 Every living thing that moveth upon the earth. God said, behold, I have given you every herb bearing seed, which is upon the face of all the earth, and every tree, in which is the fruit of a tree yielding seed to you. It shall be your meat. And to every beast of the earth, and to every fowl of the air and to everything that creepeth upon the earth, wherein there is life, I have given every herb for meat, and it was so. And God saw that everything he made, and, behold it was very good. And the Evening and the morning was the sixth day. Thus, the heavens and the earth were finished, and all the host of them. And on the seventh day, God ended his work which he had made, and he rested on the seventh day from all his work, which he had made!

Sarah Bowman

Free Love

Did you know that one of God's most significant works of arts, is you? Did you know that you were always on his mind? That each day that passes by, he has thought of you a million times. Each feature he has handcrafted on your face and spoke you into existence long ago. There is only one you! You were never a mistake. His heart is so connected to you that we cannot even fathom how much our Creator loves us.

Just as he created each tree unique, each flower with its sweet smell. He created your smile, and that dimple in your cheek, your beautiful hair. You are his greatest gift, his most significant accomplishment, his most blessed child. He loved you so much that he became flesh for you. He died on the cross and gave his own life. If you had been the only person

13

Sarah Bowman

on this earth, he would have died just for you, and he just wants to love you, he wants to hold you and cradle you. His only desire and wishes are that you would choose to love him too.

 His hopes and his plans include you; little ole you! You may think that you are unworthy of love; you may feel that God just does not understand. However, know, this is not true. You are God's, only you.

He always knew you. Jeremiah; before I formed thee in thy belly, I knew thee, and before thy camest forth out of the womb I sanctified, and I ordained thee a prophet under nations. Life can be hard, so hard to understand, I know that. There is so much pain and sadness in one's life when we refuse to allow God to speak to our spirit. If you listen, he whispers through the trees, and his love carries on the breeze. He is never too busy, to hear from you. His only wish is to hear from you. Our relationship, with God, is so unique; so special. That the world, and people around you, even if you tell them, they will never know.

Sarah Bowman

The Christian Hippie

God keeps your secrets, and your worst pain he can handle. He can handle all of you. The dark parts, the messy parts, the broken pieces, the empty parts, and the forbidden parts! He can handle them they are never too much! You can lay them down, and speak to him, cry to him.

There is no set prayer, or set way, that you have to worship him. You do not have to sit in a pew at church to know God. You do not have to wear the right clothing, you do not have to look a certain way, and you do not have to clean your face before you cry to him.

You do not have to recite words or sing a particular hymn. Your relationship is yours. Just get alone with him, make your time with him special. If you are unable to speak, he can see your heart. Ask the holy spirit to speak for you. Being a follower of Jesus Christ is not a religion it is a relationship. The most important relationship you will have in your life.

David danced before the Lord; 2 Samuel. He danced before the Lord with all his might, and David was only wearing a linen

Sarah Bowman

ephod. Other's looked at him as if he was crazy. He danced and worshipped his God, at that moment God and he was the only ones there. David was called a man after God's own heart. He glorified God, very personally and very passionately. He loved God, and God loved him.

However, his life was full of challenges, and obstacles, and sin and brokenness. He worshipped anyway. David being so small in stature, however his faith so strong that it conquered a giant! His trust not in himself, but in his God. I love to read about King David in the bible, I always see myself in him. He Loved God. However, he did not lead, a perfect, sinless life, David's words, in the book of Psalms, were him, crying out to God with all his might. I am still crying out to God because I just can't seem to get it right! What David taught us in scripture, and showed us, he was a flawed human being. David teaches us that honest selfexamination is necessary to recognize our own sin and that we must repent and cry out to our God; for the lord examines our heart and does not look upon our outer appearance. He looks at our heart.

Sarah Bowman

The Christian Hippie

David danced, he worshipped, and it was not what others might have seen as worship. However, David's heart worshipped his God! God sees more in you; then you may see within yourself! He has the keys to the darkest pits of your heart, and he being the only one who can turn the key. King David wrote most of the book of Psalms, a lowly boy; God saw a king in him. He wrote the sweetest poetry of all of Israel.

David pours his heart out in the book of Psalms to his Heavenly God. Perhaps, you are at a place in your life; you need to call out to God. Whether, you have just learned his name, or known him for years. If you feel are at a place, in your life, and that you need to cry out to God. By all means, cry out to him.

Psalms; Answer me when I call to you my righteous God. Give me relief from my distress. Have mercy on me and hear my prayer. In peace, I shall lie down and sleep, for you alone Lord. Make me dwell in safety. Lord our Lord, how majestic is your name in all the earth.

Sarah Bowman

The Christian Hippie

You have set your glory in the heavens. Through the praise of your children. When I consider your heavens, the work of your fingers. The moon and the stars, which have set in place.

What is mankind that you are mindful of them, human beings that you care for them? You have made them a little lower than the angels and crowned them with glory and honor. You made them rulers of the works of your hands; you put everything under their feet: all flocks and herds and the animals of the wild. The birds fly gracefully, knowing the Lord created them.

 Lord, Lord, dear Lord how majestic are thee. His eyes are watching over you, even when you fall. The sun was so very bright today, as I went into the woods to pray. High above the tallest tree, the sun seems it was shining just for me. I look up and what did I see, the trees and earth were smiling only for me. As I raise my hands high above, I could feel his spirit descend just like a dove. My prayer, my time, he has always been such a good friend of mine.

18

Sarah Bowman

The Christian Hippie

As a child when I would fall, he would still be there through it all. I would look to the sky for peace, and his face there I seek. I hid in the kiss of breeze, as I could feel his love and mercy flow through me. I spoke to him, I would sing to him, I fell in love with him. We have our special place, where I almost could see his face. Did you know that God seeks your special place too, as he did with King David?

The world may see just a broken, lonely boy or girl, man or woman. However, God may see a King or Queen. Seek that quiet place, when you are alone, and away from all the chaos of the day, for God seeks that quiet space deep inside of you, where you will not have to hide your face away. You can dance with all your might, before your God.

You can sing praises, in the morning and the noontime day! You can walk through the quiet forest, and seek refuge below the towering trees. You can skip, beside the riverbank, and touch every flower you see! You can stand barefoot, with your toes dug deep into the dirt, your hands held high, or your face, to the earth.

Sarah Bowman

The Christian Hippie

You can bow, stand, you can sit, sing, jump, and cry. You can feel the wind on your face when the sun is so high; you can feel the warmth dance along your eyes. As you pray, your hands folding or apart reaching to the sky. It is that quiet place of worship deep within your heart, for God seeks that lowly space, which holds all the pain that just never seems to go away. Perhaps, you were hurt, as a child, feeling as if you had no voice. Maybe, you were lonely and thought you had no choice. Worship him, just worship him. Seek his face, in a world that says you have no place. For God spoke you here, you belong, you belong to the most excellent artist, the grandest most gracious, merciful father.

The God, of all the heavens and the earth. You; he wants you to want him too. He wants to hear your voice; he wants to have that relationship with you, that personal choice, to trust him. To follow him, to know him. Seek his face, in that quiet place of your heart. God is a spirit, and they that worship him must worship him in spirit and truth. O let us worship, and bow down; let us kneel before the Lord, our maker.

Sarah Bowman

The Christian Hippie

Sing unto the Lord, for he has done excellent things, this is known in all the earth. O God thou art my God; early will I seek thee; my soul thirsted for thee; my flesh longeth for thee: in a dry, thirsty land, where no water is. Sing unto God, sing praises to his name: extol him that rideth upon the heavens by his name is Jehovah and rejoice before him.

A father of the fatherless and a judge of the widows is God in his holy habitations. Worship is such an essential part of our walk with Christ. Understanding what worship is connects us to the praises of our savior. I have set in many church services, of all dominations.

I have watched while many raised their hands, swaying from side to side. I have also, saw many who seemed to have no expression on their face. Either one is okay. Because there is no set way to worship Christ. Some people may be more private with their time with God, while some may be loud and excited.

Sarah Bowman

The Christian Hippie

Worship is personal. Perhaps, many were like I am. Many may want to sing praises and worship unto God when they are alone. I am very selfish when it comes to my prayer time with God. I admit it. I enjoy praying with other's in crowds, however, when it comes to my prayer time, I would rather be alone with God. There are some things I talk about with God, which I may not feel comfortable speaking about in front of others.

Things that many people possibly would not understand. I know God will listen, and he and I will work things out. So traditional worship, inside of a church has never been my thing. I feel closer to God, when I am away from other's, in the quietness of a green forest, among creation.

You worship where you connect with God. Perhaps, you worship God in church, or alone in your room. Find that connection with him. Do not let anyone tell you, how to worship!

Sarah Bowman

The Christian Hippie

I went into the forest to pray, away the pain from the day. I seek your face my God in a world full of monsters and chaos. Teach me, Lord, teach me to walk with you God, and in the cool of the forest allow me to hear you! The trees always feel secure, and the sun seems to speak to me.

 As a child, I would find a place to hide and spend time with God. It was just him and I. The Kentucky summers, always gave me such excitement. I would slip my shoes, off and run through the mountains. I was free when I was in creation.

I did not have to speak, I did not have to worry, and I just had to breathe. So many summers' I spent sitting and dreaming and praying. I did not know what I was supposed to be praying or saying. I did not know, what to say to God. I just knew, that when I found him, I just fell so in love with him.

 I was a troubled, worried, afraid child. I saw peace in him. My favorite place to dream as a child was on a large rock that had broken off, from larger mountains. It had broken off many,

Sarah Bowman

many years before I was even born, and made its permanent home, near my house.

So, as I child, I spent hours and hours climbing on that old rock. The sun was warmer, up there, life felt safer when I was upon the rock. I felt no one could hurt me. I was safe there. I would feel the warmth upon my cheek as I laid against it. The sun was close to me.

The sunrays would dance along the edge of the leaves, and shine on my face. I think back to the feelings I felt upon that rock, they bring tears to my eyes! I was such a broken child. Hurt, scared. I felt so alone, in a world that did not care. It seemed that everywhere I looked there was another monster hiding and waiting for me.

When I set upon that rock, I was free; I was safe. I would stand up and sing. I would talk to God, in ways a child does. So innocent and full of wonder. I would ask him questions, and I would cry. I would tell him, about the pain I was feeling, about the rejection, about how afraid I was!

Sarah Bowman

The Christian Hippie

Now as an adult, I realize perhaps, that rock represented God, in so many ways! He was stable and secure; He was warm and caring. He was the sun I was feeling on my face, as I closed my eyes. I could see the yellow from the sunrays. The rock became such a place, a place I found peace. Peace as a child of eleven, who felt they were never enough!

I was enough there; I felt strong because I was alone with my rock, my peace, my strength my God! Later in life, I would come to realize that he was near me, so much during such difficult time in my childhood. I talked to him more than I spoke to my family at times. I was so free with the wind in my hair. I did not worry when I was there, I just lived! I think I would have spent my whole life there if I could. It was a safe place.

My mind was so confused and filled with thoughts of pain, abuse, abandonment. I did not feel secure; I never felt safe! However, God always showed up to greet me, when I laid upon the rock. Of course, as a child, I did not understand it all!

Sarah Bowman

The Christian Hippie

I just know, that to find a place when you feel so alone, to find a place that feels safe, grows on you!
I do believe that is when I fell in love with the beauty of God's creation.

I felt at home, with the flowers and the trees. The grass felt safe upon my feet. Have you ever had a time, in your life you were so afraid, that you didn't know what to do? Did you have a hard time finding a place that felt safe? It may take soul searching, but look into the depth of your soul, where did go when you needed to feel safe?

Remember as a child when you would spend around in a circle trying to make yourself dizzy? I can remember laughing and falling to the ground. It felt safe there; it was solid, the earth felt stable. So much of what gave us security as a child is deeply embedded inside of us! Just a more mature version perhaps. However, as an adult that childlike worship is inside of me! The same way I worshipped a God, I just met, in a way I could not explain as small child! I just spoke and cried and

Sarah Bowman

sang. However, God understood. He understood, and still understands me, and understands you too!

I am his baby, his child. He has walked with me, through my whole life. During the lonely, hard, painful times of my life, he never left. He watched me grow from a scared child, not even sure of what tomorrow brings, to a frightened teen, which was uncertain about so many things.

He walks alongside me, as I have become an adult. However, to him, I am just his child! So, he knows, when he looks in my eyes, I am still that eleven- year- old girl. Looking for peace, looking for stability and looking for acceptance. He sees that same child of eleven in my eyes!
Because he is my daddy, my perfect God!

This is my worship with him, he knows me, through and through, he knows you, because he created you too. So, finding your worship time with God, is so very important. No one knows, the burdens you carry. They can't understand the way your heart beats, or how you cry when you feel you're alone! They see that smile you bring; perhaps they see the

27

Sarah Bowman

anger that lingers from a painful childhood. They do not understand as God does.

Because he created you, and he held you before you were ever placed in your mother or father's arms! I think we can be so caught up, in religion and yes even church membership, we forget what a relationship is with God.
There are no two relationships the same.

For God, knows your deepest pain, and all the hidden parts of your being! And he still loves us! He loves us so much that he gave his own life so that we can have peace and eternal life! As a human, it is so confusing; human love is so superficial. People just decide to fall out of love sometimes. People just decide they want to walk away, and not love you anymore!

However, that is not the way, God loves! He loves no matter what, and he does not fall out of love with his children! God just wants us to love him, with everything that is in us! He does not wish us to hurt! It breaks his heart when we hurt! He never intended on any of us to hurt.

28

Sarah Bowman

The Christian Hippie

However, sin entered in this world, and that was when people began to hurt! God hates the sin; he loves the sinner, where are you in your life? Have you reached that point where you feel, all hope is lost? Do you perhaps, feel you aren't good enough? I do not know what pain, you may have endured in your life. I do not understand how deep the pain is! However, I do know someone who wants to take that pain, away and build a king or a queen!

Think about it and give your heart a little self-examination. Perhaps, wherever you are in your life. You will find a safe place, where you can call on God, you and father can sit for a while, as you confess all your pain to him, holding nothing back! Just laying it all down, at his nailed scarred feet! He wants your pain; he wants the deepest intimate parts of you, he slowly wants to put your brokenness back together! Find your worship, with him and make it yours! Make it something that you look forward to each day! Do not look nor listen to others for that security; you will never find it there! You will

Sarah Bowman

The Christian Hippie

only see perfect peace with Jesus God's only Son, that

whoever believes in him, shall

have eternal life through Jesus

Sarah Bowman

The Monster

I wander alone, a barefoot child. Alone and afraid. So, many monsters were there; they wanted to devour me. As a child, I would hide my head under a blanket, as I just could not find a safe place. Some monsters lurked along those mountains. That when the sun went to sleep, the guilt and pain would rush over me! I was hurt and abused by a monster, that pretended to love me. He lied to me; he violated me.

The beast spoke, words that a child should not hear. He had spoken, fear into me, as I thought it was my fault. I thought it was me! The monster lived everywhere in trees; it seemed as he lurked all around me. My hands would shake, as I saw, the monster's hands reach for me. Perhaps, he will eat me. My

Sarah Bowman

innocence lost, in the perverse of his tongue. He inflicted pain on my siblings and I.

That monster that found the most vulnerable parts of us as children, that beast felt he could hurt us! I was always running, always hiding from that monster. His eyes, just seemed like they looked through me. Slowly, ripping away, any self-worth that I had, and confidence that I had that monster tried to take from me. With abuse in his words, abuse in his eyes, abuse in how he made me feel! I ran so far, into the forest. I was safe there, Safe from him, and all that he tried to take from me. I was merely a child of eleven. I found refuge among the trees, as God met me, a scared child among the leaves. I cried inside, unable to speak.

Can you see God, what he is doing to me? Can you see God, how he makes me cry? Can you see that monster, which wants to devour me? Take me, God, with thee! Show me, Lord, I am frightened. I am frightened the darkness, is too much to bear. Father meet me there. Help me heal from the anger that I hold

Sarah Bowman

within me. The violence of an abused child. As, I release, it all to thee. My Lord, speak to me!

I am alone amongst the trees, can you hear my heart weeping, as a monster comes creeping. Release the feeling of shame and guilt, my dear God. Release the pain of abuse. Release the feeling of never being good enough. I held onto these emotions and fear, for so many years! The monsters that were there to cause me so much pain! Release them, Lord, as I call your precious name. Restore me, Lord, as I once had no voice, and now I do! Guide me,
Lord, as I heal in your presence and you take, all my insecurities, and allow me to love myself! For any abuse, leads a terrible scar!

Those monsters will try to keep us there! They will try to keep you in that pain. They will try to keep you in the rain! Have you had to run from monsters in your life? As the monsters begin their Lies, they lie to the deep pain that is hidden inside of us! The monsters that live within the abusers of the past.

33

Sarah Bowman

The Christian Hippie

The monsters that want us to give up at last! However, Lord, we must not stay there.

For that pain that burns inside, will tear us apart. The monsters will try to follow us through our lives. Heal me, heal them, Lord! Forgiving the abuse of the monsters makes us free! As you deal with the pain, they caused us! For our suffering is not in vain! We offer no vengeance as you carry that burden for the deepest parts of our soul. For I cannot hold, that pain inside of me. As, you reach deep into my soul Lord, and speak to my spirit, in ways I will never know! For the healing, comes from the Lord. The pain lies to us, telling us, that we are not enough for you! The monster, the darkness, will lie to us! It will try to kill us inside!

You must, call on God, for he will fix the pain and abuse, and allow you to heal. Whatever, monster tried to hurt, you whatever sin, attempted to pervert you! You are NOT DAMAGED goods! You are not damaged from your past! That is a lie, from the depths of the monster's tomb! God offers

Sarah Bowman

rest! He provides restoration. He offers peace from the pain that you have held, on to for so many years!

You deserve to be well! You deserve peace, within your soul! Forgive yourself you can heal, do not allow that monster to follow you, all your life. He will find ways, to make you not forgive yourself! You can recover, as I have healed. Are you still afraid of that monster? Do you need to be free from the pain, so that you can live! For God waits for your call. He waits so that that monster can go away for the last time! So, you can see with bright eyes! So, you can smile and gaze at the world outside! That monster he will try to take away, your life!

As you may try to search for something to make the pain go away! Whether it be drugs, lies, sex or abusing yourself with the words, or actions. That monster has devoured so many, in his tracks. But, you do not have to hide anymore! God sees you! No matter what you have done, to try to make the pain go away! God hears YOU! God loves YOU!

Sarah Bowman

The Christian Hippie

He forgives YOU! He does not want you to be afraid anymore of that dark, evil monster! Whatever monster you face! Whether it is the MONSTER is sexual abuse, Rape, hate, Verbal abuse, physical abuse! YOU ARE ALLOWED TO BE FREE! That monster does not have to take you! And hurt you anymore! You can release that abuse, let it go! Let GOD take it!

Let him carry it! He can make the monster go away! Go to a place, that you feel safe, and ask GOD to take that monster away! Free your mind, and your spirit, so that you can be the person, which GOD intended you to be before that monster tried to take your peace! Pain is hard to heal. Giving up the pain is harder! However, you can do it! Just one day at a time and Father God will help you!

That monster is not you! That monster was not me! Do you know how much God loves you? Do you know what you can be for him? What you share, to help heal others! That monster must Go! He must flee, Call out to your Jesus! You are worth more than that monster told you!

Sarah Bowman

The Christian Hippie

For God sent his son Jesus, to die for you and me! I will pray for you my friend, that wherever you may be, that you will allow yourself to heal. Take some time, for yourself, and that you would spend some quality time with father God! The potential inside of you is limitless when God holds your hand! Join me in the garden, as we pray and ask the Lord, to take that Monster away! But the God of all grace, who hath called us unto his eternal glory by Christ Jesus, after that ye have suffered a while, make you perfect, stablish, strengthen settle you. The righteous cry.
And the Lord.

Therefore, being justified by faith, we have peace with God through our Lord Jesus. For whom shall call on the lord, shall be saved. Casting all your care upon him; for he cares for you. Here are some bible verses that will help you deal with the emptiness, you may feel inside. If you have been a victim, of the lies of the monster.

Matthew 11:28 KJV Come unto me, all that labor and are heavy Laden and I will give you rest. **Psalms 18:48** He

Sarah Bowman

delivered me from mine enemies; yea thou lifted me up above those that rise against me: thou hast delivered me from the violent man. **Psalms 22:24**

For he hath not despised nor abhorred the affliction of the afflicted; neither hath he hid his face from him; but when he cried unto him, he heard. **Psalms 9:9** The Lord will also be a refuge for the oppressed, and refuge in times of trouble

Sarah Bowman

I'm okay

I lay with my heart upon my sleeve, broken and bitter and that pain, that radiates through me. To my surprise, I believed that you would be, the most significant blessing to me! However, your existence was just a moment. Your heartbeat for only a second, as you slowly drifted asleep, far away from me. I never held you in my arms. I never kissed you on your precious cheek. Your existence never happened. I never got to watch you take your first step or even run to me, a moment in my life, where I hurt considerably, I felt completely and utterly broken. My heart was shattered, with your goodbye! My dreams all washed away, like a butterfly caught in a storm. With it so beautiful, however, delicate and deeply broken was I.

Sarah Bowman

The Christian Hippie

The pain was something I thought would go away with time, fake smiles. Hopeful tears. I begged my God, to allow you to be here. I had dreamed of you and watched you. Your beautiful hair in the suns light! You were holding my hand, as the sky passes us! The dream of lying with you upon my chest, as the grass tickles your sweet little toes.

You were a lie, you never happened. I lay alone, the day you left! I was so broken and dark that I knew I would never see the light of day! I lie in the tub, full of the blood that once gave you life! I was empty.

The pain and loneliness that I felt! Fear that rose, up in me, as I lay on the cold, dark hospital bed. Just alone, with my thoughts, my regrets, my sadness unable to be eased! I wanted you so badly; I needed you! I lay there, so alone, and afraid. The doctors told me that day; you would be not be born. Your soul had just begun to form. However, you flew away!

The moments in my life would stand still. The breeze was only offering me only a chill. The trees were not offering me a

Sarah Bowman

home; the grass just laid there all alone! The sun was still shining as my heart lay there dying! I had never known, this type of pain! I just prayed and prayed to be me again!

To be able to see the light in the sun. To be able to feel lives fun! However, I was numb. I did not feel anymore! I felt the pain radiate so much more! I thought of myself as a little child. Wishing I had a lap to crawl upon and rest my weary soul. Someone who could explain to me that you will never be! My heartbeat saw three; I felt the life die within me! Its heart no longer to beat. No sound of little feet! No running along the grass, in the summer heat! You were gone even before we would meet I held you those short moments. I talked to you; you were deep inside of me! I lay in the coldness, of the world. Like everyone forgot about me!

The life that once thrived had died within me! I gazed upon the beauty of my children's face; an empty spot now took your place! The dreams and hopes of tomorrow, slowly began to fade, as the heartbeat that existed was dismayed. The angels

Sarah Bowman

came and took you alone, to a heavenly home! I cried and cried, at the thought that we will never meet!

However, in the darkness, I felt his arms wrap around me. As I lay so still, and as I had to tell my heart to beat! I heard his voice deep within me. Saying Sarah, we shall meet, upon the seashore, you shall see, that happy baby that should make three. I lay alone, no one to call, no one who understood the pain of it all! However, I was not alone, you God said, my child, come along. I will sit with you awhile, and I will show you, it's okay smile. For the pain will soon heal, and your child is indeed real!

He rests upon the sea, the crystal blue water that flows through me! The sun will always shine on that sweet baby of mine! For he was in my plans, but his heart too grand, for a world that would not understand! I lay there alone, my family barely calling me on the phone! For God knew me, he knew that I would be, sad for a while. However, he will calm, and I will indeed smile. The sun will shine on his face!

42

Sarah Bowman

The Christian Hippie

The angels will graciously take my place, as mother and as a friend! We will meet again! For God promises me, that when I call heaven my own home, you will be there, However you not alone. You have another brother you see! For God decide that fourth baby with you will be.

Years passed my heart begins to try to heal, as all the pain was still so real. The Lord decided it was not time, to have these precious babies of mine! I know at the time, I lost my two children that started to thrive within me. They were only a moment! And then they faded away, into eternity! During that time of brokenness, I thought I could never feel again! There would be no way that I could go on! I was indeed blessed with two beautiful daughters.

However, my heart longed for those that I never held! I had never felt such loss in my life! I laid alone, crying out to God, he comforted me, and taught me, that I would live again. I will rise, and I will love! In my moments of brokenness, only God could hear me! I was angry I was beaten, I could not understand, why this would happen to me!

Sarah Bowman

The Christian Hippie

The life I had been promised will never be! The Lord helped me, during that time, in ways I will never understand. He comforted me with the sunset in his hands. He listened to my cry, and my anger he did not hide! God was aware of how sad and in despair I felt. However, he was always there! I found strength in him, and in myself, that I had never felt before. There were changes inside of me, that day that my babies went away! Perhaps, for the better, for I understood that I had no control, even if I could!

As I begged them not to leave, their soul was free! My God, he did not leave, he stood there, giving strength to me! We may never know, why we face so much brokenness and sadness in this life, we may never know, why things happen the way they do. This is where faith comes in!

Faith is something you cannot see; you can only feel it, smell it, taste it and live it. However, you can't see it! You can grow from it! And you believe it, and you receive it! I have faith that my God knows better than me!

44

Sarah Bowman

The Christian Hippie

I cannot explain to you why, and I know how bad, it feels to cry! I have been in that dark place, where I search and search for his face! However, he is not far away; he is there every day! We grow in pain, just like the flowers grow from the rain! We get stronger with each trial we face, and however, we must seek his face, the brokenness is too much, to carry alone. He must take place, of all the pain, and sadness.

For he has the only gladness. I know how hard it is to hurt, I know how it feels, such desert! However, God offers you a new day, you wake up, and take that breath of the air away! You breathe through your lungs! Your heart is a beat! You are alive, at that moment. He will be there to meet, even your darkest moments. He will hold you, if you fall, and try to make sense of it all!

I know that having a broken heart is so hard! It seems it will be in pieces, when the trial is over! The tears will eventually fade, but the memory never went away! Find God in that brokenness, when you feel you cannot even breathe, Find him, where you will, he will see! I walked along the forest the day

45

Sarah Bowman

they died. I would look up at the trees, wondering if I could see them hide! They were among the clouds and rode the gentle breeze. I woke and felt the sun upon my cheek! A kiss from my babies that were no longer within me! They were with God, and Jesus and all that will that will be!

I know, that perhaps, you may have felt a different pain, you may have suffered differently. However, our tears, the Lord keeps! I hope that you find, that moment you can speak to that friend of mine, that man from Galilee. He would love to pick up the broken pieces within thee!

He will place, them together gently; his hand carefully will build that heart again! So, wherever you are my friend! Know, that God is there! It may take a lot of time to heal, for I know, I am still not at that perfect place. I am still working on a lot of pain! I am running through a lot of moments of rain.

We will be okay, as long as God is there! He walked with me through it all and is always was there to catch my fall in ways I do not always understand. There are no special powers that

Sarah Bowman

are in my hand! I cannot know for I am just me! However, I am strong when I am on the rock! I am secure with him. He is my rock, for which I stand all other ground is sinking sand. Examine that heart of yours, give him a chance, to show you a healing that is so deep, that you can even understand!

 I hope wherever you may be in that broken heart, you may think of thee! Precious God, merciful Lord, protect them father, keep them, God, just as you hold me! Let them seek refuge within thee! Under the most beautiful tree, with the wind through their hair. Father meet them there. So, they can find you in peace! The raging of the pain, will one day cease when we look upon our savior and touch his feet!

I cannot offer you, a particular word that can make the pain, fly away like a bird! All I can do my blessed friend is offer you a beginning and an end! He will be there, as soon as you call! Just give him a chance that it all! Take that time, to walk along the shore, or touch a flower you never saw before!

Sarah Bowman

The Christian Hippie

Take a moment away, from the chaos and strife that won't go away! He will meet you where you will be. He will meet you under that tree! I can see, him through the leaves as they tickle the bottom of my babies' feet!

As they rest upon the heavenly shore, they are so much safer than they have ever been before! I know that they will know me, for when I get there, they will hold me. They will see me praising God, in all creation as heaven will my final home! Find your place, with God, find your healing with him, he has always wanted to be your special friend!

He heals the brokenhearted. My God knows my plan, and yours too! Just as I was a child of eleven, I was afraid of all the monsters that lurked around. He looked into my soul, and let me know I mattered, whatever I was going through it mattered! Your issues of pain are important to him. There is nothing that is not important to him about you! I know that some may feel God is too busy. However, God always has time for you! He wants to hear from you! So, whatever, pain that you hold inside, he cares. My prayers are with you, my

Sarah Bowman

friend. Take that moment today, if you're hurting, or sick, or angry! Take a deep breath, do you feel that air in your lungs?

God breathes life into you! Breathe healing into your soul! He can touch the parts of you that seem un-healable! He can do it! He is a good God; He is a good God even in hard times! Do you see the sky outside, can you see how free the birds fly? Look up at those trees outside, know that God is there by your side. The trees and mountains are his masterpieces.

Walk along the ocean shore, when you come back you will be different than you were before! Take that time to breathe, take that time to be! For God, waits patiently for you, to call on thee!

Perhaps, you will find him in creation like me! He is everywhere, just call upon on thee! He will answer youyou will see! Maybe, you have lost a child, like me! There is no more profound pain. However, your pain isn't in vain!

Sarah Bowman

The Christian Hippie

I pray that you find God, and call out to him so that he can pick up the pieces of your broken, heart and that you shall see your sweet baby again!

The pain started inside of my knees and slowly made its way into my body. The pain began in the pit of my belly, so much that I felt I could not breathe. From a child that was young hiding under a tree, climbing on a rock that shielded me.

 I was left in a place that was not free, for an unknown sickness came over me. I had just laid my baby in heaven to be. This illness was not of me! Perhaps, the pain was crying to be free. I did not know, what would be. The sickness controlled all off me; Food became an enemy to me!

It did not to offer me relief it did not coat the belly within me. The pain so severe in my gut, I did know, what was up!

Then came the weakness, which came over me! I was hollow, and broken and sick within me. Was this the emotional pain I held from so long ago? I did not know. The pain I feel through my feet, as each part of my body turned on me! My belly

50

Sarah Bowman

could no longer eat! For the pain from the food was too much to beat! The weakness came, in my hands, as I did not understand what his plan was!

All I did was hurt in pain, and scream and beg and call out his name. I could not stand there was too much rain; the thunder grew too much pain. I did not even recognize me! I held so much worry, anxiety from my past! Could I be crazy at last! The sickness, that raged my body made me weak! My feet could no longer carry me! I was frightened and so scared, and I did not know how much I could bear! As food became my enemy, and many did not even believe me!

I was sick, from something I could not understand. I was not sure it was in God's plan. I had already hurt so much in my heart, from children that decided to part! There was something strange, as I felt I would never be the same. My heartbeat so quickly, my body would shake. I knew that the pain was too much to take!

Sarah Bowman

The Christian Hippie

It was dark no one could see, the sickness that was raging inside of me! I could not stand, as the world spun at my feet! I would wake at night, as I crawled myself to the bathroom. I was much too weak. Who had I become, a sick person? I felt my body grow weaker, as food became so painful I could not speak.

As I ate, the food ran through me, the pain and burning shook me! Food became a fear, as the pain was always near! No one knew what I felt; I was just lonely once again by myself! The sickness invaded, my body, as I begged for it to leave! The thought of food left me. I could not eat, I only wanted to sleep! I was weak and sometimes felt too tired to speak.

The blood draws the poking never gave relief, as doctors searched from the source of what was in me! Each year, it seemed it would never leave! As even getting groceries became much of a task for me! I laid in bed, afraid that my heart would forget to beat! I was ill, and no one knew why! This mysterious illness has come over me! The words and

Sarah Bowman

explanations became too much, as I stopped trying to explain what was up!

It seems my family did not even see, that the pain was raging inside of me! Each Thanksgiving, Christmas and Easter, I sat afraid, because I knew I could not eat! Living in a world that would not believe in me! Some say it was all in the head, but I felt that with a sense of dread, for I knew, there must be a plan, even though I did not know how to try!

The moments when I watch my feet tremble and my legs too weak to walk. I feared that I would be in a chair because the weakness was a lot to bare! Each doctor, I would see, said I should not be walking, my balance so unsure! The world spun out of control. My husband fell off his feet, as he laid his hands in prayer over me! I could see the fear in his eyes; I think he was afraid that I might die!
His prayers were intense, as he carried me along!

He tried to make the pain go away, his hands laying on me!
He prayed for an answer to this disease, which had no name,

Sarah Bowman

no way to be seen. It was invisible it had not a name, some did not believe I still felt the pain, the same! I just prayed to walk amongst the trees; I wanted to feel the peace within me! The way I did when I was with thee.

The tears would fall, every day, as I prayed for God to take my illness away! Make me well, make me see, help to feel the health through me! With each pound that fell, it was a pain that would make me yell! How food could make me sick, how could I become so ill quick! It had seemed that something was invading, me something that did not want me to be free! The tears would fall, I felt hopeless and confused with it all.

Years passed by, so much pain, I never knew why! The weakest had become a part me. The anxiety of falling, where would I be! My hands were weak, my body ill! I never knew why; still! Each thought, too tired to speak!
Where I have gone, who was now! I knew I must get better I just do not know how! I had gotten to a point during my sickness I felt I may give up!

Sarah Bowman

The Christian Hippie

The dizziness scared me and made me unable to do anything anymore. I worried my children, would hate me, because I could not play at the park, with them anymore! I did not know what was happening. Each doctor gave me a new excuse! These were the sickest moments of my life; my body had given up. I could not eat solid food any longer.

So many regrets and doubts ran through my mind. I just wanted to be well. As, my body, grew sicker, my heart was so afraid, and then one-day Jesus began to take it away! I started to be able to eat small bites, and at the moment, I knew it would be alright. With more food, came more energy. Then slowly, I became stronger, trying to walk a little further, to build the strength in my body once more! There were setbacks, and feelings I felt before. However, I felt life within, as I prayed for the lord to take away this pain from me! My husband stayed close, as we prayed for a cure. We prayed for a way, a way I was sure! There was up and downs, through my seven years of sickness. The building of faith, and

55

Sarah Bowman

strength, I never knew I had! Food had been taken away from me. Normal life had been stolen from me.

However, I grew stronger and stronger in him in my health. Food began to nourish my body once more. I could feel a spark of hope within me! I had lived a lot of my life, angry with myself; the way I looked was never good enough! With each diet in my past, too thin, was a thought of the past! For health was my determination. Strength was my goal.

I became less critical of me; my health was improving. I felt like I had been walking through a dark forest, and there was darkness on all sides of me! A shadow followed me into the woods. Where there was once sunlight, had begun to fade. I had felt I was living someone else life! However, slowly, I was improving. My steps were getting stronger as, I cried out to my Lord, to heal me! I cried for him to give me my life back. He was giving my life back. He had shown me, that he did not leave my side! He slowly healed my body. He slowly, made me complete once more.

Sarah Bowman

The Christian Hippie

All prayer and praise to the king of king Jesus Christ.

He is healing where I was sick and restoring me to better than I was before, Physically, mentally and emotionally. Have you ever faced times in your life when you were so ill, you could not speak? Have you ever dealt with pain that you thought would never end? I have, if you are there, even as you read this book. I offer you some hope if you have lost all faith. The Lord still hears you; he knows your cry!

He knows you need a change in your life. There are so many types of pain, which we face in our lives, that affect every aspect of our life. I am a firm believer that stored pain inside can cause sickness and illness. Not forgiving someone who hurt you, holding anger and fear, can poison your body! Everything comes back to surface if you do not deal with the emotions.

God cares about your pain and your hurt. He cares about your fears and insecurities. He wants you to heal, in every way! If

Sarah Bowman

you are holding anger, let it go! If you are keeping hurt from your past, make peace with it!

 We aren't able to control, sometimes if bad things have happened to us. He cares about every aspect of your life. Every moment that passes by, and every heartbreak that you have ever had. To find that special relationship God is so much more than a ritualistic worship. I know, for I have been sick, and now I am well. I have felt pain, and isolation and sadness, in ways that I could never honestly explain to another human being. However, God understands.

During my illness, I felt like a tattered butterfly in a cold rainstorm, with my wings tattered down, and broken. My body was frozen and weak! However, God has restored me to better than what I had ever been before. During my sickness, he taught me to notice the small things in this life.

The way it feels to love someone, the way the trees look after a warm summer rain. He gave me new eyes to see from the depths of my heart. He opened my eyes, to the most precious

Sarah Bowman

things in life. The way warm blanket feels wrapped around your body! The way fluffy socks feel on your feet, or the friendly blaze as you sit next to a warm fireplace. The healing smell after a rainstorm.

He had awoken a part of me, which was deeper than it was before. I can remember the way it felt, to begin to eat solid foods once more. How sweet a cherry would taste. The excitement I felt to walk, even if it was a small distance, God allowed me to see that we are all broken, we all need healing and acceptance. We take so much in this life for granted each day! We often forget what a blessing it is to wake up with breath in our lungs, and a heartbeat in our chest!

Struggles are hard. Sickness is hard. Losing my children was heart-wrenching. However, he restores us, when I focus on him. However, there is a beauty that lies around us, that can lift us when we fall. God gave us so much. I know you may feel hopeless at this moment, and you may feel you have nowhere to turn.

Sarah Bowman

The Christian Hippie

I offer you a chance at this part of the book, to reflect on what is deep inside of you? Where are you? Are you broken, and feel you will never be whole again! Do you feel heavy and weak, unable to speak, unable to walk? I was there emotionally, physically, spiritually.

If you cannot walk, then crawl! Just keep moving towards the cross, and carry your hurt, pain, and burdens, to our Lord and savior. For he gave up heaven, and bled and died on a wooden cross. He loved you so much that he was sacrificed so that we can live! Wherever you are at in your life. Know that God can meet you. You do not have to meet him in a specific place; He will come to you! He can comfort the most broken parts of your being, and restore you to better than before! You are more than a conqueror in Christ! You can make it. Take your broken heart to Jesus; he will put it back together again! You do not have to remain broken forever.

There is a pain that is deep inside, a pain that we all try to hide. Perhaps, the pain of rejection, anxiety or fear, Pain of abuse, or of the darkness that always seems near!

Sarah Bowman

The Christian Hippie

Rejection causes scars that appear they will never heal.

Abuse causes belief that you were never even real. Heartbroken, that feels there is no way out. God offers you a safe place, a place to rest the weariness. He provides healing, for those who ask, he offers to heal us from the pain of the past. I ask you, at this moment, have you been hurt in ways, that words can't explain? The pain causes us to forget to see. However, we can heal. God can give us the key! We can feel again and love; we can sing his praises from above! Wherever you may be, he will be in the midst, just call out to him. He will give you peace. I am a living testimony, I have walked in the darkness, where there is no way out! I know my friend, I know. However, so much healing has taken place, inside of me, healing that God is only capable of! Have you battled a sickness? Are you ill, as you read these words? Don't give up, don't give in! Lay your pain at his feet!

Life becomes so hectic that we often forget to stop and breathe. We forget how important it is, to stop and smell the roses. During my illness, I was taught the importance of breath. Life

Sarah Bowman

had always had me running in a million different directions. Worrying about things, which I could not control.

I never realized how important it was to the body, to breathe correctly. We live in a fast-paced world; No one knows where they are going, or where they will end up! During my illness, everything seemed to make me feel awful! If I talked too loudly, it made me nervous, if I walked too fast, it made me dizzy. If I worried too much, it made my stomach hurt. My life was forced to slow down. My thinking, my actions, my words; just me, every part of me had changed.

As a child, I found quiet places, to think and to breathe. As an adult, I forgot how important it was, to find a place of quietness and peace. It was not until my illness; I touched the deeper part of me! I had to learn, to calm down, and to find peace where I was. This was very difficult for someone like me; I was rushed, with all I needed to do in a day.

During my illness, all I had was time. Time to think about the past, to try and find ways to heal what had happened to me.

Sarah Bowman

The Christian Hippie

Everything was complicated for me! So, I begun, to slow down. I began to talk slower, to eat slower, to walk slower and to be in my present situation.

I had never done, that before. I never knew how. I was thinking about the future the past, the beginning and end, with a million worries dancing inside my brain! I never realized how important it was to my body, to allow things to be! Lord speak to me in the midst of my trouble, teach me, Lord, how to breathe into you and speak life, to all that around me.

Time has grown slowly, with each passing day. The will of me is fading away. I have forgotten how to be; life had gotten the best of me. The passing of each day, teach me, Lord, to know how to be. Teach me Lord, how to allow your breath to calm me. In a world, that causes pain and illness with no name. Teach me to see, more beauty around me.

The seasons are beginning to change. The winter months blow cold through me. The spring offers hope, and summer

Sarah Bowman

provides warmth. Each year show me, show me how to breathe again. When darkness falls, like a curtain of black around the head and onto my back.

As the body begins to heal, give that strength and the will to breath. As you, give each beat and each air that passes through my lungs! I am forced to listen, dear God, I am forced to learn your ways and not my own. For I know, the reason why I lay so low, I know the reason why Lord. I had not given you all my troubles in the past. I am learning to rely on you more. The moment I closed my eyes when my child had passed. I prayed and prayed, but your will be done my God my father.

Your will with my life, with my body, with the spirit of my home. Your will be done, as you breathe your air into my lungs. I often forgot as I am now forced to listen. Teach me, Lord, how to breathe. Teach me how to have faith in the tomorrow you will bring. Bring the grass closer towards my feet, so I feel the way wetness becomes me!

Sarah Bowman

The Christian Hippie

The drops of water, as the tears ran down my feet! The moments of surrender, as you breathe life into me! Allow me to touch the Lily, to see the changing of the trees, for Lord has given that to me! For the money, can't buy, peace. Peace is only found through thee! The air smells lovely after the gentle rain, the dancing of the leaves, and twirl along the breeze. I am here Lord, I can hear you, and I can feel you! The flowers, look more beautiful with each day. My steps are slower, as I gaze around at your masterpiece. My mind only focused on beauty, the pureness of you. I am caught in a world, which seems my own. You have shown me so much.

The wonder of a child, as I see things through your eyes. My blessed God, my peaceful king! Thank you, for your life, which you have given to me. Teach me in your ways, and not my own. For my own offer me sadness, and my thoughts offer me madness. When I rest upon you, I can breathe. I can finally live, the way I want to live, praising you!

The song of the birds, never sounded so sweet, when I am weak upon my feet. The sun never felt as warm, when I woke

65

Sarah Bowman

from the pain and cried out your name! You taught me to be. I seek you, Lord, as I walk through the cold forest, with the dirt underneath my feet. I find you, Lord. I see you in the passing clouds, as you teach me. So much life had passed by me. I forgot how to see the sky! The rain came down and washed me to ground.

I found you there! For you held me quietly, I rested on your knee! Life gets so busy; we lose sight of what is important. We lose people; we lose words, we miss so much! However, we never stop, to look at all you have given us until we feel broken.

I see your beauty lord, I never will forget, the day I met you beneath that tree. When the sickness still flowed within me! Now the Lord of peace himself give you peace always by all means. The Lord be with you. 2 Thessalonians.

Find a quiet place, take a deep breath. Breathing through your nose, and slowly out your mouth. Closing your eyes, begin to meditate on what is right, and what is lovely, finding God in

Sarah Bowman

your breath. Slow down, take a moment to drink in the beauty of creation and God. As you rehearse all the blessing God, has given you. As you slowly breathe, in all that is good. The trees with their green lush, The flowers as they fragrance tickles your nose. The sound of the wind flowing through the trees, on a snowy afternoon.

Find that happy thought in your mind.

As you thank your God, for all, he has done. For we can do nothing unless God gives us our next breath. Breathe and meditate on God's goodness and grace. Slowly allow yourself to be present.

Tomorrow will take care of its self, for the Lord knows the plans. He will guide your steps, and take your hand. Find that moment with him. Allow yourself, to be happy, to smile as you think of all the blessing that he has given; it is a time to laugh.

A chance to be still and know he is God. John 16 These things I have spoken unto you, that in me ye might have peace. In the

Sarah Bowman

world, ye shall have tribulation; but in good cheer. I have overcome the world.

Philippians 4 Be careful for nothing, but in everything by prayer and supplication with thanksgiving let your request be made known unto God.

Isaiah 26;3 Thou wilt keep him in perfect peace, whose mind is stayed on thee because he trusteth thee. As you cast all your burdens on to the Lord.

You can be still, and rest upon him. He knows the rising of the sun; he knows the name of the highest mountaintop. For he spoke the world into existence. Resting upon the rock, the solid rock of God, leaning not in our ways, but his, he lives within us. Our Lord, our God, our perfect peace!

My dear friend are you weary, from your travels, has the moments just became too much to take? Is life rushing around you? There is peace. Peace in an instant if you take the time, to breath and spend some moments with God in quietness.

Sarah Bowman

The Christian Hippie

For God is in the garden waiting for you, he is waiting for his time with you. Wherever you are at, what pain, that may flow through our weakened veins. Rise, and rejoice in the Lord he hears your voice. In the midst, of our storm, he will hold you and keep you warm. Find him, seek him, and cry out to him!

Sarah Bowman

Fog lifted

The leaf slowly cradles the earth, with its delicate broken frame. It sways along the gentle breeze, along the windowpane. The tree begins to look bare, as all the leaves have found a new home along the chilled ground. The breeze is chilly as the leaf gently fall. The earth will soon, prepare for the fall rest. With the winding down of the grass, and the ground shall sleep a sweet slumber. The tree appears broken and somewhat in wonder, for the beauty that was on it, the earth shall now share. Have you ever felt beautifully broken? So much beauty, however so much brokenness. How can God, love such a sinner as I.

How can he want to save a broken person?

70

Sarah Bowman

The Christian Hippie

The sin has made me dirty, and the sin has caused a glare in my eyes, my heart cries to God for forgiveness. For I am just a lonely vessel, floating aimlessly upon an isolated sea.

No one can see me; I am in a fog, perhaps forgotten in the thick smog! There is pain hidden in the depths of me. We all have sinned and fell short of the glory of thee. No not one is righteous. Only Christ.

However, the Monster tricks us into guilt, and covers with the deception like a thick quilt, each sin he lays before us. Each lie, each deception he reminds us. He speaks with his eerie voice, telling us we have no choice.

Whispering in our ear, he lies to us. Speaking doubt, anger, sadness, guilt, abandonment over us! He speaks in a loud voice. He speaks lies, telling us that we are not good, enough, that God could never love a sinner. That your sin is too much for God to bear. He lies, his lips are deception. And his eyes, speak desolation. The monster tells us that we will never be

Sarah Bowman

forgiven. He speaks pain and deceit, over us, as we fall deeper and deeper into our sin!

We will never be good enough to pay our sin debt! It does not matter, what you do, you will be able to be good enough to pay the price for your sin. Our actions will never be pure enough. For our flesh and spirit will never walk as one! They fight among each other, every day of our life. Your works, will not pay the price. Your money is not needed here, for God sent his son Jesus to pay the sin.

He knew we could not be good enough on our own; he knew we would fall, we would be broken and too weak from the fall. So, Jesus took your dirty, filthy sin he took it all! The lies, and fear, and the pain that is so near! And he left it on the cross! You cannot be anything without Christ! The monster will trick you. He will convince you that your actions, determine your salvation! We do not determine our salvation.

God never asked us to save ourselves. He never asked us to fight this sin alone! The sin is much too much to bear without

Sarah Bowman

The Christian Hippie

a savior. Each sin that the monster has up his sleeve to throw at us, we are not strong enough to fight in this life without GOD! For the monster comes to steal, kill, and destroy you, he is a lion seeking whom he may devour.

He is confusion; he is the perversion that spoke on the lips of those who hurt you! He is confusion; he is the delusion. He is the pain, the monster, in the darkness, that lurks in the night. He is self-loathe, he is depression, he is anxious, he is fear, he is unfaithfulness.

He is the destruction of marriages; he is the center of racism, he is hate! Every word, that the monster speaks, is negative, he not of the light! He is suicide; he is pain that will not go away. He is the one, which tried to ruin you! He is the one, who is the enemy of all! The monster is a liar. You are worthy of forgiveness; you are worthy of love from a perfect savior.

GOD, gives us the strength to keep fighting, he is the comforter. GOD is our strength He loves you so much. The monster will cause you to become so spiritually broken, as he

Sarah Bowman

tears down your confidence he will tear down your worth! He will convince you that you are nothing! He will keep you in your sin; he will try and suck the joy, and happiness out of your life!

You are beautifully broken, my dear, to the Lord, cherishes you! No sin is too strong for God! No matter, where you came from, there is hope only in Jesus Christ. Nothing will fill the void in your life! No one will be able to make the pain go away!

Only Christ knows how to make the pain go away and never return! You do not have to carry it alone, the heaviness of your burdens. You do not have to pay the sin debt for your sin! For God, is the only one that holds the key, to happiness. He is the only living God. He will fight for your brokenness, he will plead for your heart! He will cry with you when you cannot speak.

He will lift you when you cannot walk! He will carry you along the troubled waters if you allow him to. You can be free

Sarah Bowman

from all the sin; you can be free from all the pain, just call out his name! Plead the blood of Jesus; it washes you clean!

You do not have to feel guilt or shame anymore. You do not have to feel confused about the way to go! Nothing that you have ever done will keep you from becoming clean! Believe in the Lord Jesus Christ, and you shall be saved! You will be made whole, through him! You are his most prized possession. He can defeat the monster. He can make you strong. For God, knows your name, you are beautiful in his sight. Can you not see? You do not have to be alone! You do not have to fight the battle, for he hung on that tree and died for YOU and me!

Close your eyes, my dear, take a breath. Remember you are enough for God! Are you lonely my friend, have you reached a place, in your life that you don't feel beautiful in God sight anymore? Are you in a haze of depression and sadness? Are you weak from the lies of the monster? Has the monster defeated your spirit? You can rise again, my dearest friend.

75

Sarah Bowman

The Christian Hippie

For God says, the monster must flee in the name of JESUS!

You are clean!

Sarah Bowman

Beautiful Love

And he shall be called beautiful; he shall be called the advocate. He shall be called the resurrection. He shall be called the life. Jesus shall be named the Sheppard. He shall be called the bishop. He shall be called the judge, He shall be called the man of sorrows, he shall be called the head, and He shall be called beautiful. He shall be called master. He shall be called faithful, he shall be called a friend, he shall be called a faithful witness, and He shall be called the rock. He shall be called the high priest. He shall be called the door. He shall be called the living waters. He shall be called the bread of life. He shall be named the Rose of Sharon. He shall be called the Alpha and the Omega, The beginning and the end. He shall be called the true vine. He shall be called LORD.

77

Sarah Bowman

The Christian Hippie

He shall be called the Messiah! He shall be named the teacher!
HE shall be called the HOLY ONE! He shall be called the
mediator. He shall be called the beloved! He shall be called
the branch. He shall be called the carpenter.
He is the good Sheppard. He is the light of the world!

He is the image of the invisible God. He is the word! He is
chief cornerstone! He is the savior of the world. He is a servant
of God, He is the author of our life, and he is the finisher! He is
almighty! He is Faithful. He is merciful; he is humble. He is
the almighty, everlasting father! He is Shiloh. He is called the
king of kings! Is the great I am. He is the called the Tribe of
Judah. He is the prince of Peace. He is the bridegroom. He is
the only begotten son of his father GOD! He is a counselor! He
is called Emanuel. He is called the SON OF MAN. He is called
the dayspring! He is called the AMEN! He is the KINGS OF
THE JEWS! He is called the prophet. He is our Redeemer! He
is the anchor that keeps us from sinking.

He is the bright and morning Star! He is the way the truth and
the life! He is Jesus Christ! There will be many different

Sarah Bowman

struggles and trials we all face. This world is very unfair, at times. The things we endure in our life may take your very breath.

There may be many times in your life you will feel like you don't know which way to turn. The lord has taught me many things, during my journey. He is always showing me.

I hope that you can find rest in the Lord Jesus Christ. I hope you can begin a new journey of discovery in each chapter of your life, as we are all writing a beautiful book. Each chapter good or bad needs to be included. I wish you peace.

Sarah Bowman

Love Yourself

Begin to love yourself. So many moments in my past, I forgot how to love myself. I have looked at my face in a mirror a million times, rehearsing the hurtful words. Words about the way my hair looked, or perhaps words about how chubby my face was. My poor body has heard years of heartbreaking things. I have carried four children inside of me. I have walked through sickness, pain, and sorrow. I have been strong, and I have been so very weak. I have ridiculed myself, I have called myself names. I have looked the scale and cried. I just couldn't seem to feel good about myself. I have picked each flaw apart as if I was trying to create some other person! There were moments in my life; I couldn't forgive myself. There is a time when you just have to begin a relationship with you!

80

Sarah Bowman

The Christian Hippie

You have to understand that God made you the way you are!
There will never be someone just like you. You are an original.
I am not sure if you have ever hated the way you looked, or
perhaps compared yourself to someone else.

 I guess I can speak for myself! I have been kind of bad to
myself! God began a good work in me, long ago! I was just so
broken inside that I couldn't recognize how truly special I was
in God's eyes! It is easy to be so hard ourselves! We all are
beautiful flawed; God is beginning to heal broken parts, of me
inside, he is started to remove the darkness from my eyes. I
spent countless amounts of hours just sitting in silence.
Hoping to get to a place in myself, as I accept me! Every
stretch mark, every inch of me! The Monster tries to trick us,
as he lies to us, about our worth.
So many women feel, there worth lies in on the outside.

So many feel they will never be pretty enough, or good
enough, skinny enough.

However, our Lord thinks we are remarkable. He thinks our
eyes, are the perfect shade, and our smile is radiant!

Sarah Bowman

The Christian Hippie

However, sometimes we listen to that voice of self-doubt!
That voice that tears apart, instead of the voice of God. You
see, the outer appearance, is merely a shell of who we are.

The more we build up the spiritual side inside of us.
Something, miraculous takes place. We then suddenly, begin
to see ourselves through the eyes of God, each flaw in our
outer appearance is canceled away when we are at peace in
our spirit! The Lord wants us to be-be at peace. Peace at how
we see ourselves. He wants us first to seek him, and build
from there! There is acceptance as you begin, to see the
beautiful parts of you! Each flaw is made pleasing in his sight!
You will begin to love yourself. Speak words of happiness
over you! Begin to see how much you are in God! each
beautiful mark upon you is placed because of your
uniqueness.

You are a limited edition. You are something wonderful.
The Lord can begin to change the way you see yourself! Speak
words of healing over that body of yours. Words of
encouragement, words of strength. We are strong in

Sarah Bowman

The Christian Hippie

Christ.

Begin to love your imperfections, and accept the parts of yourself, that have been so beautifully broken. Each mile you have walked, each tear you have cried, shows strength. You are a warrior of God. You are enough for him.

Speaking words of hate will only fuel hate! Speaking words of love will fuel love! This world is scary at times, sometimes monsters lurking around the corner! However, stand up, dust yourself off and begin to see God inside of you. His creation is beautiful and flawless; each flower is unique and perfect. You are his creation. When the Lords sees you, he sees beauty; your relationship grows with Christ. As you begin to work, with the holy spirit cleaning out the cobwebs, and the pain. Each pain, leaving a small scar.

However, God begins a good work inside of you. Your eyes will appear more beautiful when you love God and yourself. It's okay, to think that you are something special, you are far

Sarah Bowman

more beautiful than a ruby. Your eyes, shine brighter than a diamond.

Women who find peace within from God are unstoppable. God knew, that important role, we as women would play! He knows, the insecurities we all carry.

How about learning a little about yourself? Maybe, take some time to focus on you and your gifts from God. Spending time, with your God, and seeing yourself as he sees you! There is nothing more powerful than self- love, and acceptance of your imperfections. For the Lord takes you as you are. He holds your hand, as he helps to find the significant parts of you! The physical body will grow old, and the years will bring silver in each hair. The years of love will be all over your face. Each wrinkle is representing a full life.

Each sleepless night, as you held your child against your heart, will one day show on your face! Each line, of self-discovery, will show through! This is beautiful, this a gift! Each trial we faced, we show in our wisdom, it will show in

Sarah Bowman

our faith! Each tear you cried, will show strength within each line.

This is a glorious gift, we have loved in ways, that took our breath away! We have wiped tears, and noses, and held sick loved ones, as they cling on to us! Our babies have seen us live, and laugh and smile! You see my beautiful friend. You are so very blessed! With each year, that you blessed with, be good to yourself, speak love to you! You are so worthy of for my lovely friend. So as your youth begins to fade, with each moment, drink in the beauty of life. Dance in the rain, hold hands and hug! Be courageous and passionate. Love without delay! Show people your smile, bless many!

Walk in love, life, and truth. Forgive yourself, make peace with all those monsters in your life so that you can feel the warmth of the SON, upon your cheeks. Make peace with the imperfections, which are perfect! So, you can twirl in the rain, holding the one, you love!

Sarah Bowman

The Christian Hippie

There is peace my friend, God offers peace! Peace from within, peace with your looks, peace with your family! He offers forgiveness and acceptance. You most precious pearl. The Lord loves you. He desires for you to love him to learn more about him! Take moments to laugh, even if you want to cry!

Take moments to get to know, that beautiful woman inside, you are strong, you are worthy and courageous, you are a unique vessel, A beautiful dancing princess!
Because Your father is A king, you see! You are a princess. Find some time for you; you're worth it. Be you, be wonderful!

Who can find vitreous women? For her price is far above rubies. The heart of her husband doth safely trust in her so that she has no need of spoil. Strength and honor are her clothing, and she shall rejoice in time to come. Her children arise up and call her blessed. Favor is deceitful, and beauty is vain, but women who feareth the Lord, she shall be praised!

Sarah Bowman

The Christian Hippie

Freedom

I look to my God, for the hope of tomorrow, as each tear he has held deep inside of him. As I fight to become the women that God intended me to be. I fight all the monsters and devils that are trying to hold me down. All the disappointments. Fear doesn't define. Have you seen the road that I have traveled? For I am not there, that road is behind me. There is a beautiful road before me, that is lined with fresh green, and beautiful awaken flowers. The pain that the monster tried to build within me is behind me. As, we walk forward, in our life, remembering our path well. We may never forget, what brought us here! We may never forget the darkness that once followed.

Sarah Bowman

The Christian Hippie

However, we stand now, united. We look ahead. We are not defined by our past. We are not the mistakes that we made. For we have been made new, in Christ! The road was dark, and there was loneliness.

There was sadness, and that monster tried to devour us! However, we are not there anymore. We may have walked through fire, and had to say goodbye, to many that we loved. We have failed and succeeded. We have loved and lost! We have begged for understanding, on our knees, not understanding why! We are not weak, we are strong, for God has made us strong! We have hurt, and we have been wrong! We have sinned, and we have been made strong! For God holds us in his hands. You are not damaged because of your past! That is a lie, from the depth of the monster dark hell! We are not what we look like on the outside. We are not the size of our body! We are interwoven with the beauty that is around us! The grace of God, and his creation. We are united with God. We have worthy of his love, and forgiveness.

Sarah Bowman

The Christian Hippie

We are the dancing leaves and the fresh air that washes over us. As the beauty of person, God is creating in us! The beauty is becoming so much more than before, as you begin to surrender it all to him. For our God, knows where we have been! He knows the road, has been hard and long!

Surrendering our life, to the one who made us whole! Surrendering our pain and sadness and rising again! We are surrendering to the will, of the highest God! Surrendering to his ways, at not our own! For your path led you here, it led you to God.

You made it! You survived the abuse; You survived the hate, you survived the fear, you survived the tears, you survived the trial. You made it here! If you made it to God, crawling,

You made here! To the place inside of you, that you must now surrender. If you have been holding on to that pain, for years, if you have been holding on to your shame, if you have been holding on to the tears. This is the time, to surrender. The pain

Sarah Bowman

is heavy, and you may have held it for most of your life! Let it go the burden is much too much for you to carry.

You are allowed to be free! The monster doesn't define your steps. He doesn't follow you, anymore! Let him leave! Tell him to flee. Just let go! For don't you know the lord, planned you? You weren't a mistake. He cried when you cried. He wept when you wept, as he kept a jar of each tear!

For the lord, knew you well! I can't try and understand fully, why so many have to be hurt by the monster! I do know that there is healing! There is healing in Christ; there is healing in creation as he shows his faithfulness in all the green! For God loved you, so much that he sent his only son to die!

You can't hold the anger inside anymore; you deserve freedom! You cannot let the monster to take any more of your life! God, wants to bring you to a place of freedom! Freedom to laugh, Freedom to smile, freedom to dance before him, Freedom to twirl as we did as a child!

Sarah Bowman

The Christian Hippie

Freedom to live. You have the freedom of Christ! You can be happy! You can be content; You can be accepting of yourself! Freedom, precious freedom that is offered through your relationship with the creator, the King of Kings and the Lord of Lords!

Raise your hands in freedom, my friend! You have made it!

Rest upon that beautiful tree, or sit next to that beautiful stream. Look up, look away off in the distance, as you view all God's creation. As, you drink in the beauty of acceptance and forgiveness, and healing!

Stop and listen to the sound of the earth, and all that God has given to you! For the trees, know the song of their God, for the mountains know the tune of their God! There is beauty everywhere around you! A place to pray, a place to sing and dance, a place to worship! It is everywhere!

The holy- spirit breathing the comfort through you, as your heart and soul sing out to your God! There is forgiveness. There is forgiveness, for the dirty, there is forgiveness for the

Sarah Bowman

stains! For God, gives you a new song! Your song to sing, your hymn. For forgiveness is where all the healing takes place! Forgiving yourself, and asking God to forgive you.

Walk in the light, my friend. Walk in the sun, for you are forgiven and a new creature in Christ! All things made new. For the holy spirit lives deep within. Have you reached that place in your life, where you are just ready to surrender? We can give up all the pain, and sadness and begin to walk a new path.

 A path full of sunny days, smiles and lots of hugs! Let go and let God, become your rest. Let it all go and dance in the sun's light. With freedom, strength, peace, and harmony.

Allowing yourself, to finally rest, Surrender and find the goodness in life. Your walk may have been hard, and long. mine was. However, the Lord is still working on me, to make me what I should be! Just the words from a wandering Christian Hippie like me! I wish you peace and grace my friends.

Sarah Bowman

The Christian Hippie

Sarah Bowman

Printed in Great Britain
by Amazon

79912898R00054